The Things I'm Scared To Say

Alexis Myles

The Things I'm Scared To Say copyright © 2022 by Alexis Myles All rights reserved.

No part of this book may be used or reproduced in any manner whatsoever without written permission except in the case of reprints in the context of reviews.

Imprint: Independently published

ISBN: 9798363403378

*i dedicate this to the lonely girl,
dancing under a full moon,
hoping that some day
things would get better.*

Preface

The hardest part of beginning this piece was overcoming a voice in my head that told me there was no point in doing it. A voice I would, at one point in my life, drown out with substances, but I am approaching this project from a sober lens.

I suppose that adds more to the drama behind a title like "Things I'm Scared To Say." The nights I have spent facing myself were most horrifying. There was no hiding from the truths I expertly ran away from in the past; no safety nets were in sight.

Those who know me think of me as remarkably candid about whatever I'm experiencing. They consider it a superpower, my vulnerability, but there is much I have discovered and am still discovering about myself that I have never said out loud. Not even in a diary entry.

So what better way to let those truths come out than through a book to sell on a public platform? Though I consider this more like a school project that only a select few would see. It is refreshing how little I care about capitalizing my work in this instance since it's so ingrained into the lifestyles of modern artists. This is an act of making for the sake of it. It's a way to help me cope with the life of isolation I'm currently living.

It started with a question, "If you died tomorrow, would you be at peace with everything you did?" which was met with a "No." Too many dreams I had yet to achieve. My Broadway calling is being in a movie or publishing a book. A couple of those things could still be in the pipeline, but a book felt like the most direct thing I could contribute to. The something I could be the most in control of.

A curious thing, control. I've spent most of my life lamenting how little of it I had. With each year that passes, I remember a sure thing from my childhood that upsets me, and I hear the same mantra that's supposed to help me "You were a child that was out of your control."

Each step I take in writing all these pieces leads me closer to the truths I have been procrastinating on finding. Or perhaps, I was actively avoiding them. With all this time I am spending alone, it becomes more challenging to ignore reminders—the signs.

When I peeked behind the curtain of my habits, I could see how poorly put together they were. How things I thought were healthy turned out to be the most dangerous addictions out of all of the ones I have had in my lifetime. After seeing the raw, ugly truth, the hardest part is choosing what to do with the knowledge. How long could I watch myself continue on this path of self-destruction before I inevitably brushed elbows with suicide again?

Thus, this book. It will not solve my financial woes nor bring me the desperately desired relationships. This will only bring me closer to myself; it will show me that I can complete something that doesn't need to be executed in a new way. It is intimidating to take on a task like writing a book when you have no idea where to start. Let alone writing a book with the subject matter surrounding the inner crevices of your psyche. Sometimes I would be frozen with fear because I do not think I am at a certain "level" or artistic ability.

I am stuck on a merry-go-round of my limiting beliefs. I am not good enough, deserve to have bad things happen, and must suffer to make art. How vehemently against happiness I am; must be why I pour so much of myself into other's stories. In my mind, mine is already complete. I will drift alone on an island until I breathe my last breath.

That's heavy to hear. It's heavy to say.

But despite the beliefs holding me hostage, I understand that by talking about them, I can better understand why I came to think this way.

This book is an act of catharsis,
may this poetry bring me peace

I.
All My Ghosts

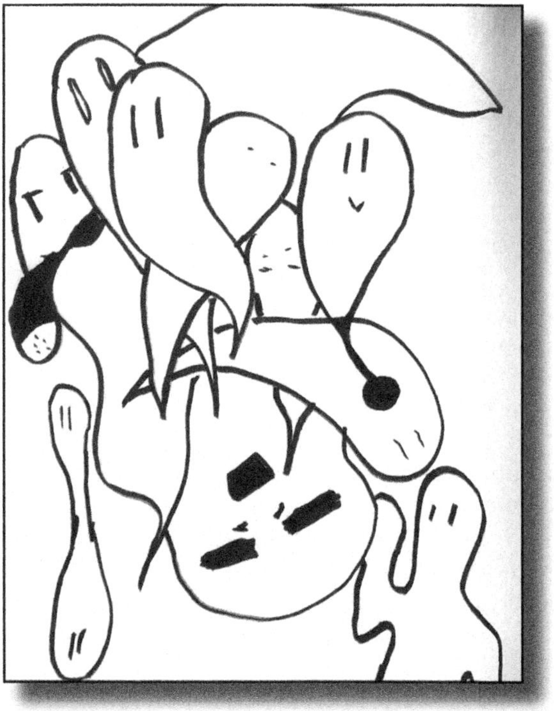

Cornell

the first time i met him was with the cops. surrounding our front door,
ready to react-
as if he was riding in on a white horse to save me from the "horrors" of
my mother

but he was the horror all along

i may not know much about him,
but what i know is enough for me to say
that he can stay as far away from me as possible.

this wasn't about abandonment,
this was about seeking refuge. safety.

i felt it in my mother's body language as she spoke to the cops about
what he did.
i saw the distance in my sister's eyes as she watched from the other side
of the room.

i believed their memories as i hesitantly embraced him and his honeyed
words about fatherhood.

promises he'd never keep.

just birthday cards with money slipped inside and a message saying
"dont tell your mom, this is for you"
because that was his narrative-
it was all *her* fault i wasn't in his life. her greed tore us apart.

and nothing could touch him with his new relationship with God
who forgave him for the secrets he couldn't utter to anyone else.
the secrets left as scars on the bodies of my family members.

i can go the rest of my life without seeing him again.

but--
he taught me something valuable.
he taught me that there are limits to love,
and loving him is something i can never do.

A small, broken family

we represent a compass,
for all our lives have gone in different directions.

i can't recall the last time we were in the same room together.

i am unsure if we ever will.

what i am sure of is, there will be the biggest void inside my heart where all of you once lived.

i will always be in search of a version of our life where we were happy,
where christmas felt warm and safe,
where the house on sparta way was never lost.

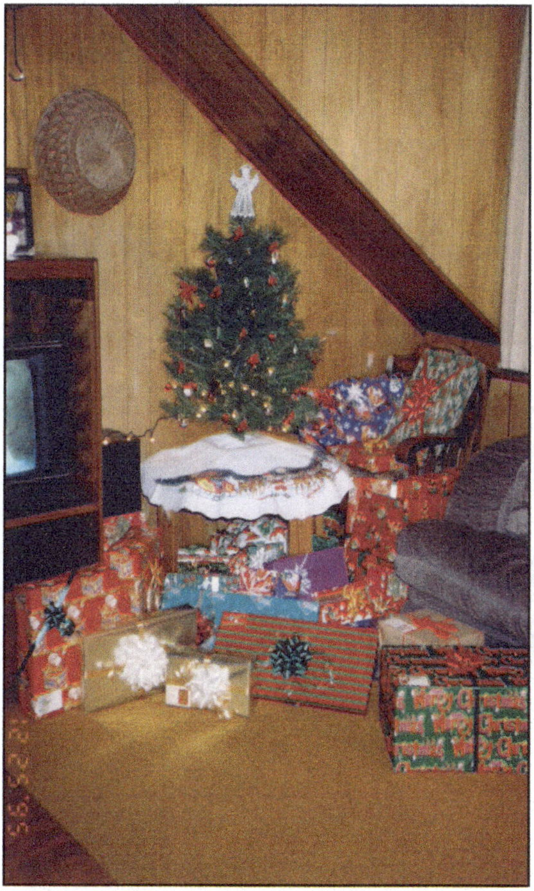

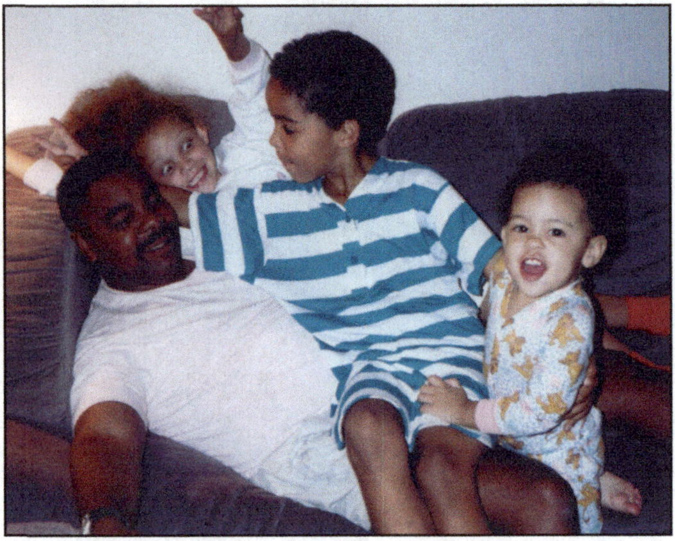

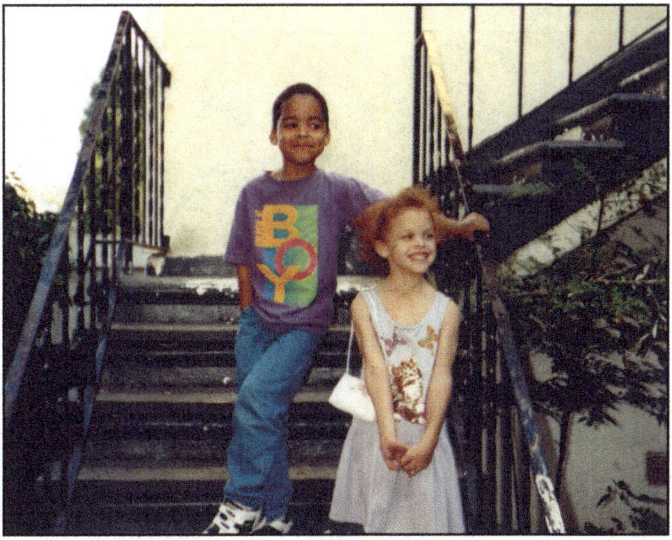
BOY

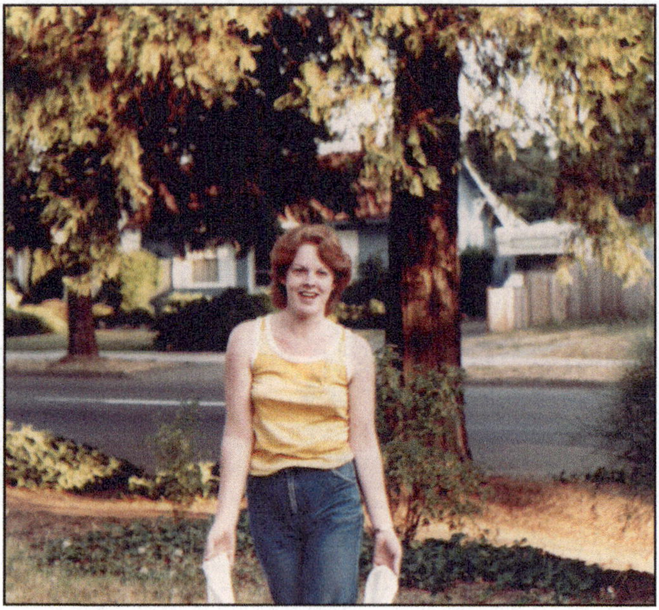

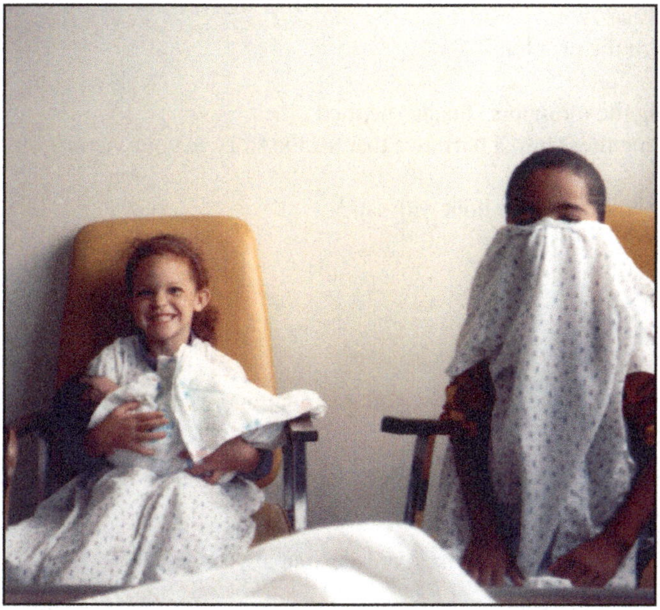

Mean

instead of hearing
"you hurt me"
you heard
"you're the problem"

taking the moments i finally snapped
twisting them into a narrative that fits the story of your victim complex

your half-truths are built with sand
once the tide rolls in,
it will crumble

erode

like all of the memories i've stored in my mind where you uplifted me
loved me
defended me

now i'm just "mean"
because i won't let you treat me like that anymore.

I'm Still Complete

I gave you everything I had
and then
you couldn't decide

so I made the decision to leave

the street in the mist
gave me clarity I thought I'd never get

and with each step I take
I find im already complete

without you,
i'm still complete
without you,
i'm still complete

on the street in the mist
im walking on air 'cause I have all I need

so when I fall in love again
my heart won't be compromised

without you,
im still complete,
without you,
i'm still complete

Universe

I felt your planet come into the orbit
The closer you walked toward me

We existed in a galaxy with complex constellations that illuminated our skin with each kiss.

A shiver ran deep through my spine touching your skin,
Remembering how vast our universe was.

Oh, how I missed the crystal blue in your eyes the most.

These are our celestial bodies,
Coming together once again,
But in a new form.

Then as you left my side,
Phone in hand to speak to the new love of your life,
You did not leave the galaxy as you did before,
You found your orbital space in conjunction with mine,
And decided to stay.

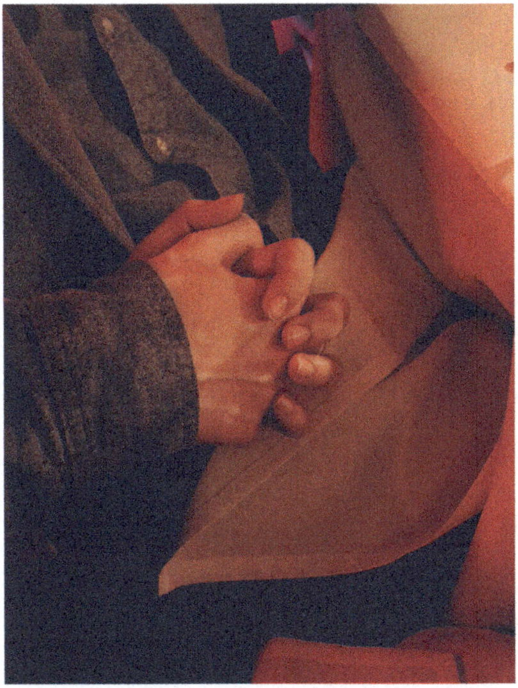

Danger

It creeps up behind me.

My mouth wanting to form the syllables
"I want you"

But you were careless.
The way things went made a reunion between us too complicated.

So how unexpected it is to see you again,
to hear you say how much I've changed you.

In a milisecond I fantasize about the idea of "us"

I grin from ear to ear when you say you feel the same.

Am I breaking a law?
Is it safe to feel joy?
No, not joy-- It's...hope

But hope breeds shame.
I hear my ghosts reappear
of unrequited loves.

Can they reciprocate?

The anticipation of holding your hand gives me energy,
gives me meaning;
then something tugs at me.

Ghosts are shouting--
~~I don't feel worthy.~~
Will they care for you?
~~The screams are getting louder.~~
Will they care for you?
~~Back and forth, I cannot waver.~~
Will. They. Care. For. You?

Now here I am,
alone in a crossing.
The wind is loud,
I'm tired from running.
This road has led me back to you–
~~that must mean something~~

Will you care for me?

Let me get this off my chest,
before you disappear again.

I can't quite put my finger on it,

But I think... I'm in danger

JJ

He called himself JJ, but maybe it was an alias.
He was 24, I was freshly 18-
He was studying to become a teacher,
I had no idea what I was doing with my life

The formula was the same.
He'd ask me to come by on an afternoon he wasn't in class.
I'd come by to read beside him while he studied. We liked to let the tension build between us before anything happened.
I remember how long his hair was,
The way his glasses sat on the brim of his nose.

He was my sexual awakening even if even difference was inappropriate.

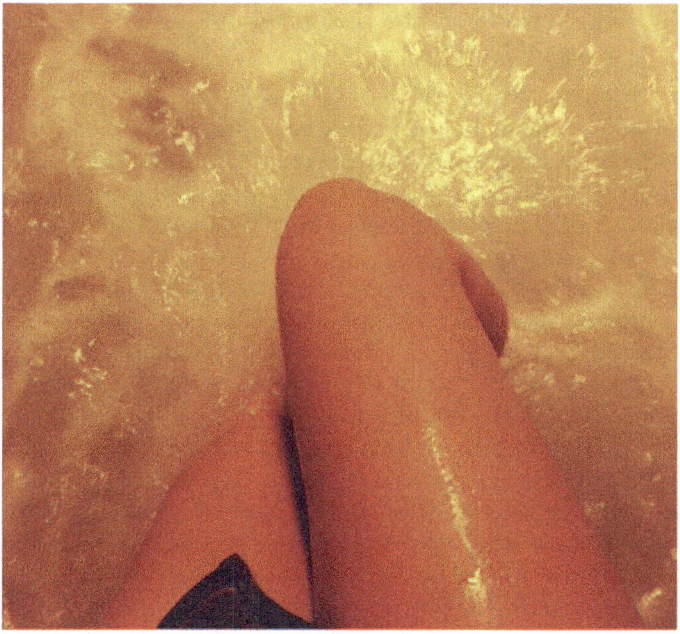

My relationship with sex doesn't exist.

After many years of thinking I have liberated myself from the tumultuous ups and downs of my formative years surrounding sex and relationships, I've realized that I have it all wrong. Let me explain.

I hit puberty at ten years old. I was shooting up like a beansprout ahead of most of my classmates. I was starting to be treated differently by boys in my neighborhood- especially on the hot summer days by the pool in one of the many apartment complexes I lived in Las Vegas. I was experiencing hyper-sexualization; in some cases, adults attempted to groom me via the praise I received for looking and "acting" grown up

That went to my head as I hit my teens. It was like receiving an award by being perceived as "mature." I felt as if I already had an old soul, but just because my soul felt old didn't mean my brain was fully formed enough to act appropriately like the adult I thought I was. That became something I could only understand when my prefrontal cortex fully developed.

I had no north star for sex education. I was a part of a family that was lost in their addictions; we never had a chance to dive deep into anything related to relationships. So with that limited view, I let many people get away with weird behavior.

It also stifled how I was able to interact with people regularly. The glances of judgment and whispers behind my back when some felt I was getting a little too "close" with someone. Being practically ostracized from my high school choir/theater group during my junior year because of my apparent crush on a more "popular" figure forced me to hide parts of myself. That any feelings of affection I have could only be expressed behind closed doors.

Though I had moments of inappropriate sexual conduct against me in my teens, I consider the first time I had sex with JJ- a poem you just read. When I met JJ, I was putting out craigslist ads to meet people (this was when OkCupid was in its origins- not many were using it at the time). Again, following the theme of keeping things behind closed doors. I considered it my first time because I was attracted to him. Before, I would be drawn to the attention given to me. That was the only time anyone seemed to care about me from my point of view.

So, it became very addicting to be sneaking glances or being touched when no one was watching. But I failed to realize how bad the power dynamics were in those situations.

I fantasized about being this mature, gorgeous lounge singer with many lovers. A being so in charge of her sexuality, I was attracted to having that powerful energy. After JJ, I found myself floating around, trying to find more moments where I could feel like the lounge singer. Unfortunately, that journey led me to be raped right before my 21st birthday. I wanted to write a poem about it, but it was (and still is) difficult to poetically describe that experience. I blamed myself for everything that happened. I put myself in that position, being alone in his house. I played along because I was afraid of his size. I didn't know I could say no even if my clothes were already off. I wasn't taught anything about how this was supposed to work. We watched a movie called Akira that night, and it was ironic to feel the same desperate pain and rage those characters went through– though I couldn't muster up the courage to scream alongside them. I can never watch that movie again. I get triggered by anyone asking me to have a movie night at their house. The event came and went, leading me down a spiral with alcohol that I can touch on in a different essay. I desperately wanted to leave the place I was living and find myself in the arms of others where I could be more in control.

Then came New York.

There was a window from ages 23-25 where I would sleep with someone new every couple of months. It was refreshing. The late-night meetings, the peaceful uber rides home where I fell in love with the big city skylines. My lounge singer fantasy was becoming a reality, but it wasn't always fun. It was only fun 20% of the time. There were so many complications with these men emotionally. My favorite clusterfuck of a situation was a man who was in his mid-30s, in an "open" marriage but had zero capability of establishing boundaries to the point where I had to yell at him in a park about how my asking to see him again should not be considered a violation of his boundaries. I have a very implicit bias against men in "open/ethically non-monogamous" relationships because it feels like an excuse to fuck other people with no strings attached but with an advertisement of more emotional availability than they're capable of.

Anyway, his wife got pregnant, and we stopped talking. I hope they're still together.

By the time I was 26, I had completely slowed down my revolving door of lovers. Too many bridges were burned, and I never felt satisfied. Only a few of them were able to get me to orgasm. That's when I started to focus much more on my self-pleasure. I felt like I was finally beginning to liberate myself.
But throughout all of this discovery, there was something following me. I often mistook it for logic, a shield, but it was the thing I always feared- just never acknowledged. *Shame.*

Shame crept its way into my bed every time I had a visitor. Anytime I penetrated myself with no one watching. My ears burned when Shame whispered to me to let me know what I was doing was wrong. It made me remember the hushed whispers from my childhood—the glares from adults when I was a little too expressive with my loving energy. Shame is the most extended lover I've ever had and the most tumultuous one of all.
I recently sought out someone to connect with sexually for the first time in over a year. It all happened over text, but the act of exchanging photos and my being fully present, consenting to the moment, caused the shame to rest itself in my stomach. I felt sick. But what was wrong? I wasn't in danger; the person on the other side was normal and age-appropriate- why did it feel so bad?

Perhaps the shame is leftover from all the memories of my past. Maybe I was running away from it, and if I tuned it out long enough, it would eventually disappear.

It hasn't. There are too many layers to this subject; ignoring the unsettling feelings won't solve anything. I must trace the shame back. I must trace it to the moments when I was a child and remind myself that what happened to me was not my fault. I trace it back to the girls I would glance at in passing or the ones I shared secret kisses with when we were alone at the playground. It stems from how religion skews our view of sexuality, and our "individual choices" contribute to our retribution as sinners. Though I never subscribed to any belief specifically, being punished for acting upon urges was frightening because breaking rules, even from a moral perspective, was not something I ever wanted to do.

So that's how I moved into the world. Too many parts of my identity have been shoved so far into a box that it was as if they never existed in the first place. I was a husk of a person- and in that incomplete state, I hallowed myself out until there was practically nothing left.

I talked about my attraction to women, and I never acted upon it despite the close encounters I found myself in. I fall more deeply into this genderless, queer identity. Still, the sexual partners I seek out reflect those who abused me, and there is no liberation in trying to fuck the echoes of those men in an environment of my choosing. It will *never* feel right with anyone until I've taken the time to work with Shame.

The key to my freedom rests
in dismantling my deeply rooted mindset.
My liberation will come when I reliquinsh my shame.

II.
Death

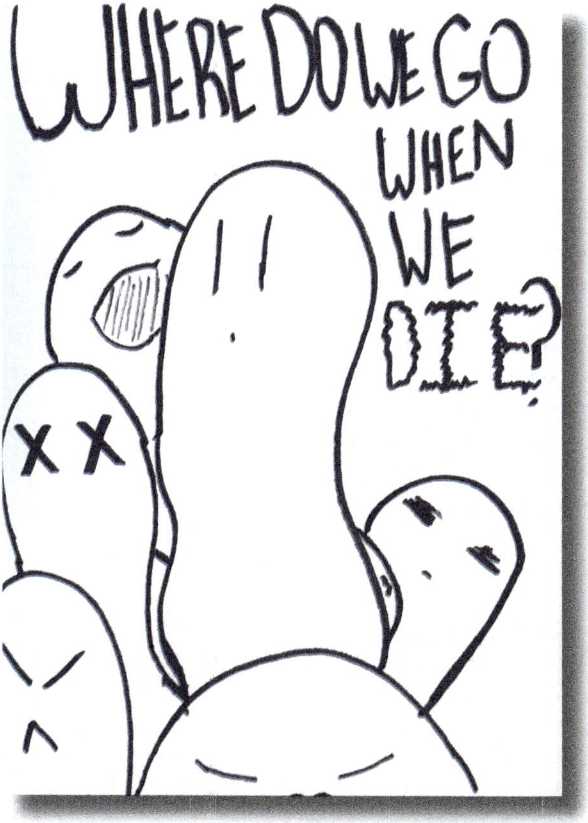
WHERE DO WE GO
WHEN
WE
DIE?

Mirror Images

A man hangs over the edge,
looking down at the Hudson,
saying 'I gotta face my fears.'

A bag by his side
not sure if it's to sink or swim

But I stand there frozen
as he jumps into the deep;

And I see myself in his place
down in the water.
This stranger and I
are mirror images inside our minds

Helicopters overhead
patrol cars rushing down the path
just to save one lost man.

And he sits in focused peace
as if his job ain't over yet

Then I see myself in his place
down in the water.
This stranger and I
are mirror images inside our minds.

I know where he's been.

I know where he's going--
he wants to die

...dontcha?

I know where he's been!
I know where he's going--
he wants to die
.....and so do I

That's why I see myself in his place
down in the water.
This stranger and I
are mirror images inside our minds.

Don't leave me alone

i dont know why you dont pick up when I call
i just want see how you are

when I hear your voice it feels real
and I'm not trapped behind a screen

(that's a facade)

dont leave me alone.
its been rough lately,
and I dont know if can handle letting one more person go

im so lonely

don't leave me alone
don't leave me alone
DON'T LEAVE ME ALONE

...pick up your phone

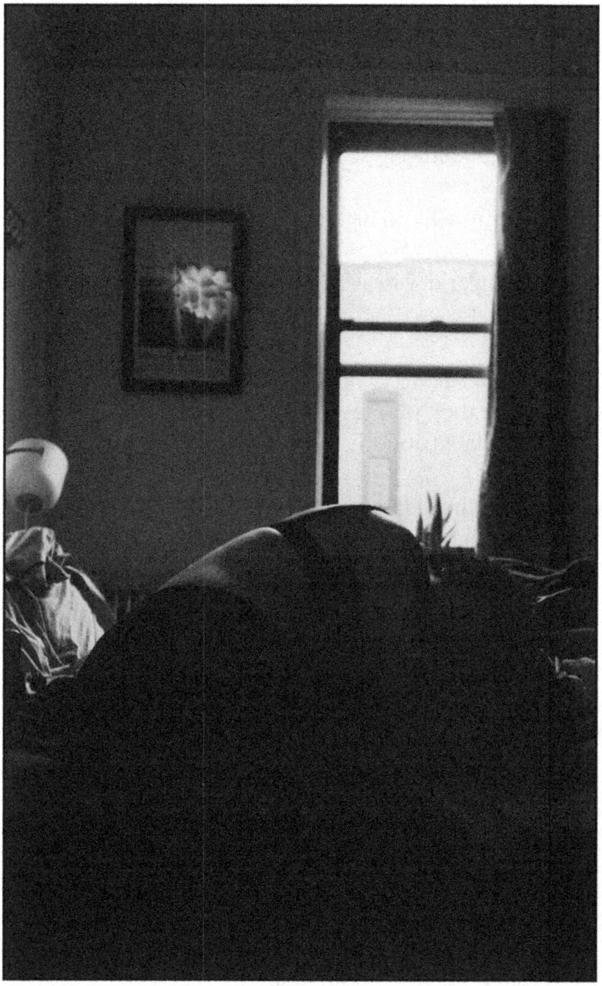

The Noose

i used my favorite headscarf at the time.

i debated how the following scene would go:

my ceilings were much too high to make a rope long enough to snap my neck,
i settled for the taller doorway instead.

i was left alone,
ostracized once again,
no one picked up their phone;
this was the last viable option

my rage built up when i fastened the fabric around myself,
i wondered why i had to suffer like this.
what kind of sinning did i do in a past life to deserve it?

on the chair, i took one more stock of my life.
i figured my roommates wouldn't find me for a few days.
maybe they would contact my mother;
perhaps no one would shed a tear

sometimes i dream about the asphyxiation
how almost immediately i grasped for freedom,
the terrifying reality that i could die—
was i ready to die?
did i think this through?

eventually i found my way to the ground,
slamming my fists against my head,
i sobbed into the ether because i begrudgingly chose life.

i chose to try one more time.

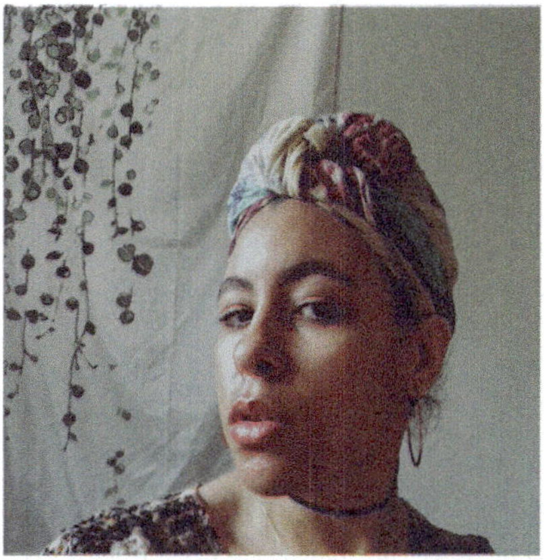

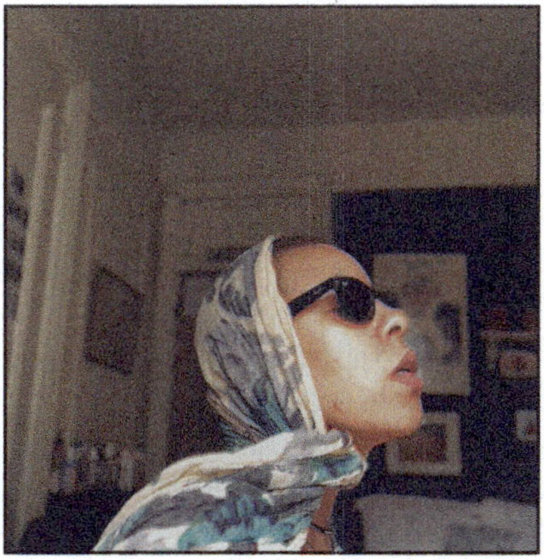

Casually Suicidal.

I wanted to write about my relationship with death from a safe place, but I find myself stopping and starting this piece due to my conflicting feelings happening every time I sit down to begin. When my world becomes challenging to manage, I believe it would be easier to die than continue to meet in this place that isolates me from the rest of the world.

The first time I tried to kill myself, I was fifteen. I wasn't successful; I was a bit naïve when I tried to swallow a bunch of ibuprofen and thought it would do anything more than give me some stomach issues. Still, the motive was there. My mother and I were attempting to escape our problems in Las Vegas in our new yet familiar home in Eugene, Oregon, where my mom spent her formative years. Unfortunately, as soon as we arrived, we were met with conflict after conflict. It stockpiled on us so heavily that I had finally reached a breaking point after moving around every few months for the past few years. We had no support system, and I felt powerless as a minor because I could not fix it. I had to go to another new school and act like everything was fine. I skipped class that day and attempted to write a suicide note, Imogen Heap's "Hide and Seek" blasting in my ears because it was the only song I could listen to that helped me feel anything. I chickened out, and the one person I texted was able to get in touch with my mom, and eventually, the school caught wind of the news. It blew over quickly; I received very little assistance and went on with my life as if I had never felt like ending it.

A running theme throughout my life was compartmentalizing my emotions. All of them. It was "easy" to deal with me when I was docile and made myself as small as possible. I wouldn't learn until later in life how those emotions don't disappear when you shove them aside. It seeps into your muscles, twisting into knots, so there would be outbursts when you least expect it as a physical button gets pushed. Years' worth of not expressing yourself makes those outbursts feel so overwhelming, but it wouldn't have been as intense had there been space where I could express myself without being labeled as a bitch.

Such a favored insult by people throughout my life, especially when I felt frustrated. Which led me to the second time I attempted suicide. I was raped the summer before I turned twenty-one, and the community I was a part of at that time was tumultuous. I knew it wasn't safe to talk about my experiences out of fear someone would drunkenly yell at me to stop getting upset about something that had nothing to do with them, but somehow there was someone that took my rape and made it about themselves. I was fragile, and the only way I could ease my sorrows was through alcohol. I could drink legally, and I would spend every weekend at the bars attempting to wash away the shame I felt. There are many days I do not remember, but a feeling that always lingered was a familiar one I had experienced just years before.

What if I died?
What if I could go to sleep and never wake up?

One night I had too much to drink, and all of the buses were done running for the night. My home was only a few miles away, so I decided to walk, but halfway through my journey, I started naturally swaying into the street. My eyes filled up with tears, perhaps because I knew this moment of numbness would not last very long. I could hear the echoes of my peers I had judging me; I could remember the screams from the movie on that fateful night when everything changed. The cars that passed through the street were minimal, but one off in the distance came towards me, and an idea came to mind. I moved into the middle of the four-lane road and waited for them to hit me, not realizing that they would likely have seen my position before they could collide. I was sobbing as the car slowed down to meet me. A woman popped her head out the window to ask if I was okay. Her tone was gentle, very different from what I was used to experiencing. I said nothing, all I could do was cry as I collapsed on the ground. She stayed with me and maneuvered a couple of cars around her so that she could continue to help me as best she could. Eventually, I could tell her where I lived and was driven home. I stumbled into my room and fell asleep as I always did on the floor. I never saw her again after that day. Sometimes I wonder if it was a dream.

After that incident, the thoughts would come and go as I experienced more ups and downs in my early to mid-twenties. My last physical attempt of suicide was four years ago- an attempted hanging after dealing with yet another social group that betrayed my trust, and I had isolated myself. Though this time, I didn't have my mother to speak to about it because it was the first time she and I had a fight and were not talking to each other. I consider that the most intense attempt because it was an act of violence that almost took my life.

But by that point, I had realized that I had yet to understand much about my sadness and the ebb and flow of the emotions surrounding it. An acknowledgment was necessary to know that the events of my childhood were not normal, and what I expected to help me deal with those situations at the time was enough for me then. But now I was older, I could make decisions that were not possible for me as a minor. The rocky waters I was traversing slowly became easier to tread. It comes with getting older, with experiencing similar situations multiple times so you can see them for what they are.

I woke up after trying to hang myself and vowed never to go down that path again. I will die when it's my time. And I was good on that promise for a few years until about six months ago. A fire in my apartment building caused me to lose everything, and the PTSD from that situation has kept me in a place where I've isolated myself from the outside world. It didn't cross my mind that although we spend most of our lives learning from the trauma inflicted in our childhood that we would continue to experience new traumas as we age. This was the first time something directly happened to me that I didn't know how to deal with healthily. I did what I knew– compartmentalize. But after a few months of looking for ways to escape my emotions, they poured over me, and I began to think about whether it would be better for me to die.

I am unsure if you have casual suicidal ideation that lasts fifteen-plus years the mindset never entirely goes away. I wonder if it's simply a part of who I am now, and it will come up when things get particularly tough.

Some days it does feel more comforting to think about ending an existence on a planet where I have only felt safe and accepted a handful of times—being in a world where I feel like a cog in a machine that has no empathy for my sadness. My worth is derived from my labor, not my ideas or emotions that don't favor the status quo. It can feel like a battle to allow myself to exist without shaming myself for not behaving in a way that the world wants me to.

But here I go again, emphasizing how the world perceives me and how harshly I judge myself in their stead when I underperform. The projections of my abusers and the rules set by our society have kept me in a death grip. They still have their claws dug into me. It makes me terrified to take up space and act like myself, which could be why death feels so much safer than being alive. At the very least, my soul could be free to transition into a dimension where I wouldn't feel persecuted every moment like I did when inhabiting this body.

How do I know death would bring me that peace, though? Every time I stood on that precipice, I asked myself that question. I negotiated what staying alive could mean to me, to my mother, and what kind of life I could live because I'm an adult and have the power to do whatever I want. But that *grip*; I am at war with projections, but luckily I have preserved and chosen to live every time it is presented to me.

I don't know if I'll ever give in, but on the off-chance I decide to end my life, I hope my loved ones remember me every time they hear Nat King Cole. Or they feel me at the tail end of summer as a breeze lets them know the fall is coming.

For now, I choose to live; I will continue to wander down this path to see where it will take me, and I will do so without bottling up my emotions. Perhaps that's the key to all of this.

To break free of my desire to die, I need to be myself unabashedly.

III.
Finding my way back to myself

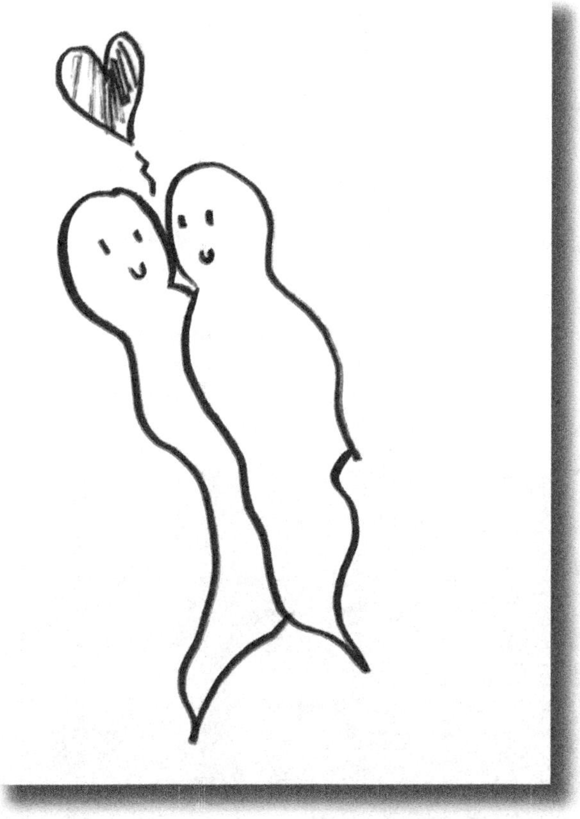

Fresh Start

mid afternoon rain at first of spring.
the smoke billowing out in a thick cloud from my lips

all the while contemplating my purpose.

perhaps there are hidden truths I have yet to uncover

and the idea brings tears to my eyes--

i realize i have options;
which connect to reasons for my life to stay intact.

In between the avenues

i wove my way through each new avenue i discovered
find bits of myself in the doorways i passed.

different version of my life flashed before my eyes,
as I walked passed each doorway of a brownstone i'd never live in

it was fun to imagine,
to escape;
and in its own way,
tell me that I can have one of those fantasies come true someday

To all The Places I've Wandered Before

Washington Heights, 2019

Washington Square Park, 2019

Riverside, 2019

Harlem, 2019

Oregon, 2015

Oregon, 2015

Oregon, 2015

Riverside, 2018

Upper West Side, 2018

Upper West Side, 2017

IV.
But who am I....really?

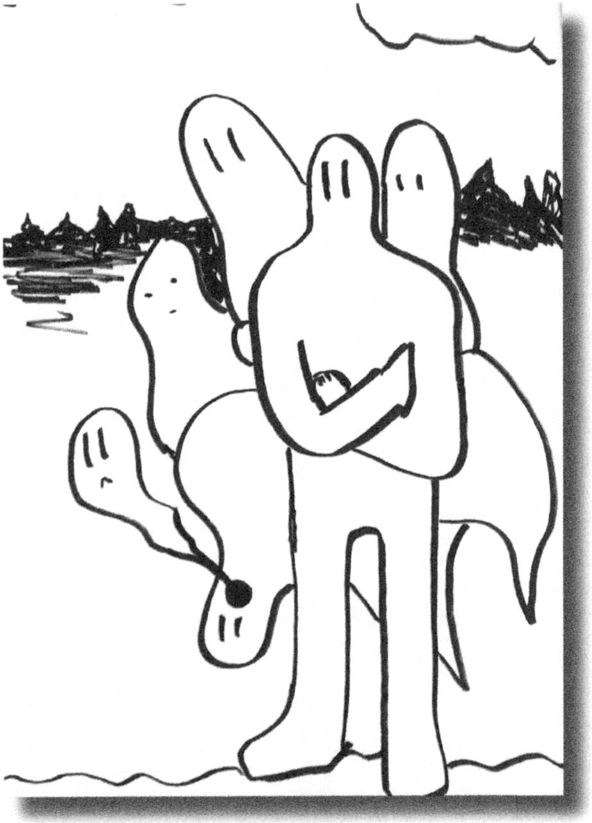

Jordan

my mother carried me the way she carried my brother
my body was big, her belly reached downward
implicating that i was to be a boy

there was no need to check,
and with glee, my little family decided to name me Jordan.
upon their excitement seeing this baby come into the world
they were shocked to see...me

different parts, and a different name

 its a story that always haunted me.
when my sister would point out in an excited tone
"you were supposed to be my brother!"
or address me by the name i was supposed to be given
i never knew how to feel.
it turned into an apologetic experience
since i didn't have a choice in how my body was made

made me wonder if i needed to transition
and complete the picture my family made me out to be

an outcast with the wrong parts.

little did i know, i was gonna carry that weight
the weight of not being Jordan

The Fire

my body aches.

/

i've resorted to sleeping on the floor to deal with the panic attacks
because when i close my eyes i hear myself wailing on the ground,
kneeling in broken glass,
as the building went up in flames.

and then, a part of me died

i had a funeral alone at the beach,
to thank the part of me that protected us for many years.

it was her time to rest.

she didn't go quietly,
she thought she had more work to do.

my love, the greatest gift i can give you
is the break you've long deserved.

it's my turn to take the wheel.

To Be Understood

i will never forget the way their eyes glazed over as i spoke.

it was never about understanding me,
it was about what they wanted from me.

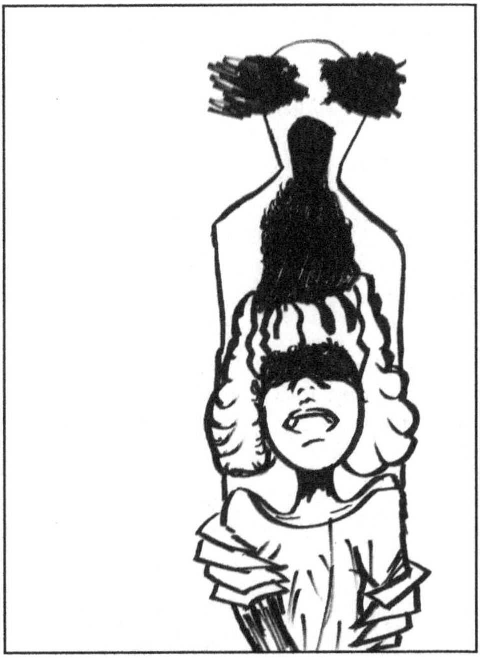

please, be messy

far too long spent in the trenches of perfectionism causes a nuclear meltdown when i make a mistake.

But does the world end?

Can I use the bitterness I feel when someone wrongs me and can continue to live their life as if nothing happened to make a sweet tonic to cure this perfection curse?

I put shackles on my ankles in place of my abusers,
due to internalizing the ways they puppeteer me to do their bidding,
and now I am my captor

please, make mistakes. please, be messy!
there is nothing to learn when one cannot allow themselves to do anything less than "the standard."

change your mind every other week about something,
let your emotions come out, and apologize if you accidentally hurt someone you love.

There is so much to discover in the spaces when you embrace the full spectrum of your humanity,
including the things that you were once ridiculed for.

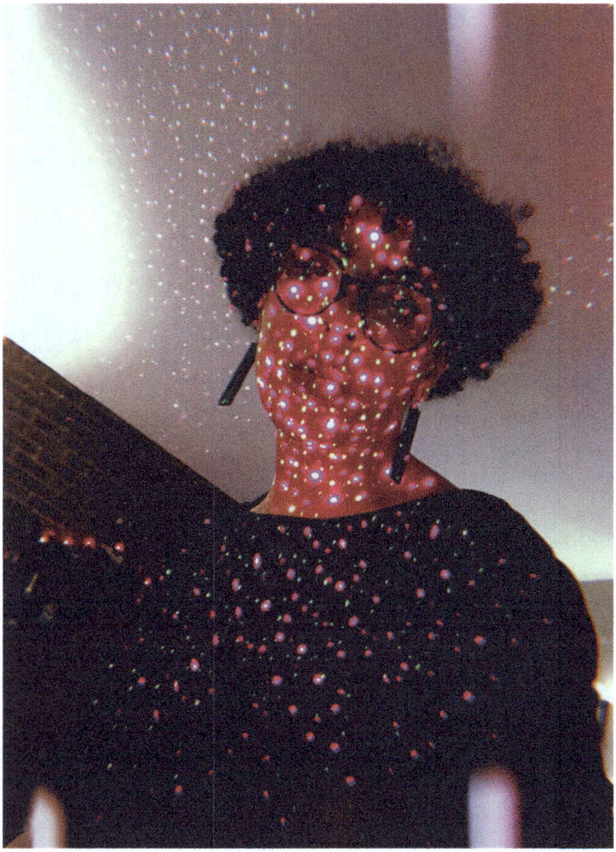

just take out the trash

too many voices piled on inside my mind,
caught in a loop of executive dysfunction.

I figure if I continue to do nothing that everything will magically be
fixed by something else

then more things pile up on top of each other,
the voices become louder and louder—

but then....i breathe, and they stop

there is no rule book for taking care of yourself.

just take out the trash,
that can be enough for today.

i don't have all of the answers

it used to feel like i was failing when i couldn't find a solution to my problems

but some things are meant to be left behind, to remain broken.

not everything warrants an answer--

including my own conflicting feelings.

Do it for Kayla

Kayla dreamed of making it to New York,
and most of the pictures I capture here,
I take them for her.

Our relationship was special,
two artists who admired each other's work so fondly
and the images we created together are the only memories I have left
of her now.

I wish I had more to say–
I wish we had more time,
I wish I told her how much I missed her before she passed away.
Only days after that last exchange we had she took her life.

I hope her soul is at peace.
I hope she looks down on me from time to time,
and sees her influence in all of the pictures I take.

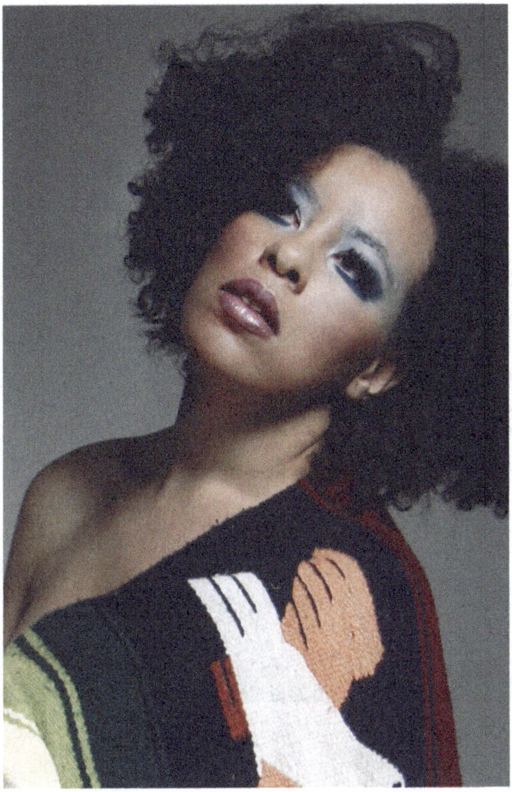

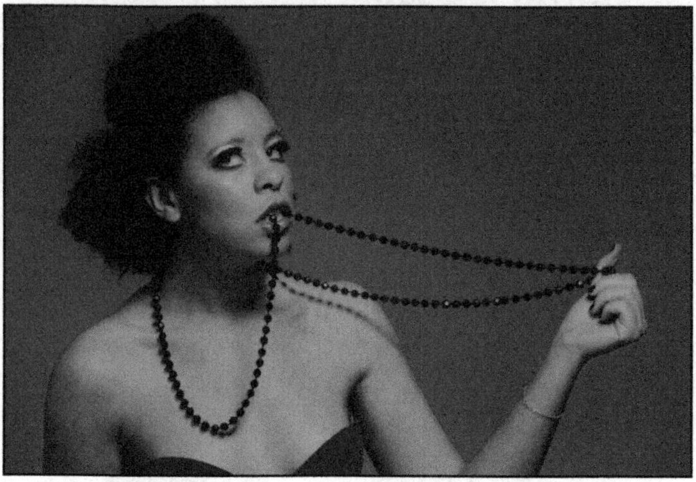

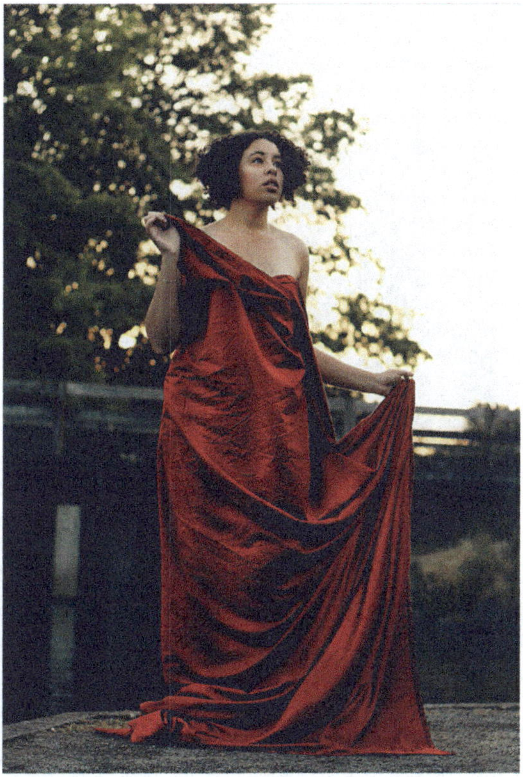

In Loving Memory

Of the incomporable
Kayla Renee Martin

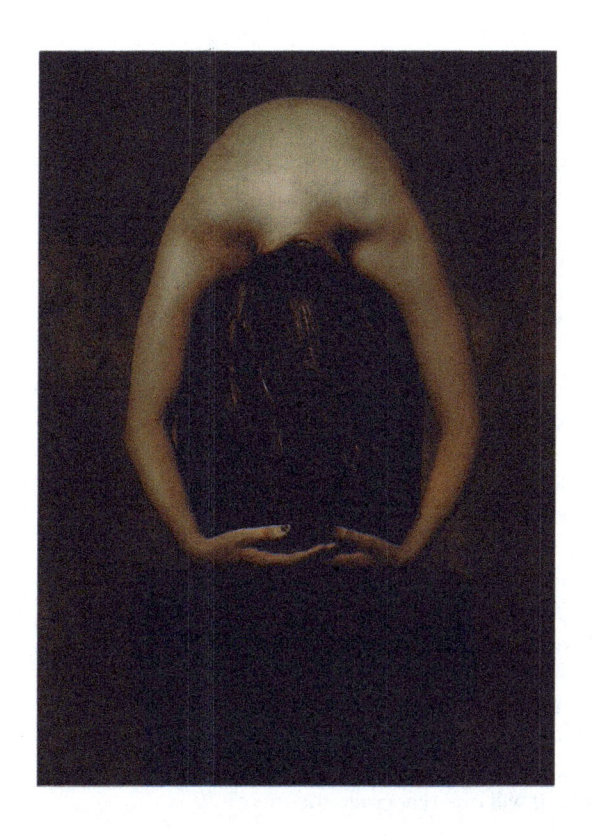

the love wound

it's easier to get worked up over the disconnection from a boy,
than to explain the sorrow of losing a friend.

the conditioning to uphold romantic love as the standard disillusions us
to the layers of heartbreak we can feel.

when it feels like no one loves you,
any rejection ripples deep into your body.
i often feel like i've been kicked in the chest,
winded,
unable to, or rather ashamed to, admit that it hurt me when someone
treated me carelessly.

my conditioning led me to believe that our capacity for pain is limited,
that our hearts only have so much room.

it made me addicted to praise,
to wildly fantasize about futures with anyone who wanted to spend
more than five minutes with me.

there is an obvious wound here,
and instead of dressing it,
i gaze upon it. i feel nothing.
i wonder if it will one day consume me.

they always sound better in my mind

i let my imagination fill in the blanks.

i find comfort in someone's potential.
let my mind mold them into what i want-
so when it comes time for them to leave,
i retreat into a fantasy
where i'd never be left behind

29

Never thought I'd be alive to see this day.

Lately my songs have been dull,
I lost my ability to string a melody

Lost so much of me, I can't tell what's left

The weight is gone, that's a relief
But days keep passing and I'm aimlessly wandering

The fog is thicker than ever
My only company is the echoes of stories from the past

Not as hurtful as they used to be, though
Things sound clearer than before

But what does it all mean?

How many years do I have left to inhabit this body?

Old, sensitive soul,
Less afraid to admit that I want to be loved

Lately I've dared to hope that it's possible
Feeling ashamed to think it's possible

To want someone to look at me and their breath is taken away
To be invited into inner sanctums and precious moments in their life.
To be held with intention,
My heart, my body, my mind

How many years do I have left?

Guess I don't need that answer today
Maybe I won't get that answer at all

Dear Me Ten Years From Now

I am writing this letter from the year 2022. By the time you read this, you've entered your final year before your forties. Isn't that wild? I hope you've stayed alive enough to read this and reflect on how far you've come.

    Every day since I turned 29, there has been a feeling in my stomach that there will be a change for the better. Though, the climate of the world at the moment is constantly at the forefront of my mind. It seems like I'm becoming much more aware of everything. How people communicate, how *little* they understand each other, and just how little power I have to change anything outside myself.
    That last part is a good thing. How many years up until now did I spend carrying the weight of other people's lives? I hope you've continued to distance yourself from the rhetoric that you must solve their problems to be loved.
    Lately, things have been foggy. It's like I'm living the same day repeatedly; I can tell I'm missing something, which is why the days seem to repeat themselves. Maybe it's the realization that I don't have a lot of faith that my life will be better. Where I can have a successful career as an artist. The ripple effect of constantly being in unstable living situations from childhood has bled into how I see our future. I say this, but the fact that I am aware of it must mean I am setting down the foundation for you.

    Where have you traveled? How many gorgeous kitchens have you spent time in to cook for yourself? For loved ones?

    Speaking of loved ones, I also realized how difficult it is to connect with people. It makes so much sense in context to our attempts at forming relationships and how often those connections ended in a way where we were blamed for things that were blown out of proportion. It comes down to us spending a lot of time with people who didn't like us all that much. We were tolerated, and in turn, we took behavior because we didn't want to be alone.

Loneliness......do you still feel that way? Well, I'm sure you do, but is it as intense? Some people genuinely like you, and I am starting to see the distinct difference between people who want to connect with you and people who like the idea of you.

It's evident how people perceive us, but now is the time to take ourselves out of situations where our needs won't be met. It's okay to not respond to everyone, to spend time with someone who you can tell is lonely but who never asks you a single question about your life. You can advocate with someone you want to have a better relationship with. The right people will hear you. The right people won't blame you for "ruining their life" simply because you want to hold them accountable for hurting you.

I hope you've found love. Love from others, but most especially from yourself.

Which I hope means there haven't been more suicide attempts. I know I have said this once, but I hope you have continued to choose life despite how hard things feel. The past is simply that— "the past". The work to uncover the parts of our trauma that have been buried is beginning, and I hope that it continues. I feel like I am starting to understand who I am more with each passing day, and though I don't have the answers to questions like "How am I going to eat this week?" or "How the fuck am I going to pay rent?", I at least know that everything I am doing is for the sake of what I need in the present moment.

Are you still writing? Are you still singing?

Creating has been so difficult for me lately. I often cry when I sing because I am unsure if I will ever get to do this as a job. Music is essential to us; telling stories is at the core of our being. I toy with the idea of stopping altogether and finding another type of work that can stabilize me financially. The Industry feels so gatekept that I'm unsure how exactly I will get in. But there is a part of me still willing to do the work, believing I can succeed.

I hope that our career has shifted in the direction where we are surrounded by trustworthy collaborators and projects that help us understand what it means to be human on a deeper level. That's in the artist statement we wrote, remember? "I am committed to making a word that uncovers what it means to be alive." Don't lose sight of it if you're feeling lost. I hope the memory of this time when I feel hopeful can bring peace on the days you know what to do.

There are many more questions I could bombard you with. How is mom? How is Pippa? Where are you living now? Even though I won't get those answers until the right amount of time has passed. I know you will make the decisions for your life that are best for you. Hopefully, mom will live long enough so you can take her on vacation or perhaps be financially stable enough to have her not work two jobs anymore. I know being able to provide for yourself and your loved ones is significant to you. It can happen. It will happen. No matter how much tar you must walk through to get here.

Life is so mysterious; it is only when we can take the time to look at the past do we find the most profound discoveries. What else will you have discovered by reading this letter? I am excited for you to continue to age, find communities you can be a part of, and do whatever you can to make a difference in the world.

Most importantly, I hope you can have more joy in your day-to-day. Days where you can dance around a home blasting music that gives you an unshakable urge to connect back to little Lexy. Each time we are loud without shame, we tell someone to fuck off and deflect their labeling us a bitch; we defend that child who had no one else to stick up for them.

I do not doubt how strong you have become over the past ten years. I believe in everything you have done and will continue to do as you walk through life. If there is no one in your corner, know I will always root for you. I will always be there with my hand on your shoulder to help you understand that life is worth living.

Keep going.

With all my love,

-Alexis

fin.

Acknowledgements

To all of the friends who have listened to me cry. For giving me the space to be a human without punishment. To my mother, who persists and hopes things will always be better despite everything. To Ray Virta, who saw the artist in me and challenged me in ways no one else has. The same for Janet and Joe. To the crew from Las Vegas who showed me that love can still be evident even with years of no contact. All of you have contributed to nourishing my soul, allowing me to defy the standards I had set for myself and become more well-rounded. This book has given me catharsis, and it won't be the last that I write.